The Life of a Caribbean
PIRATE

by Ruth Owen

Series consultant:

Suzy Gazlay, MA
Recipient, Presidential Award for Excellence in Science Teaching

Ruby Tuesday Books

Published in 2015 by Ruby Tuesday Books Ltd.

Copyright © 2015 Ruby Tuesday Books Ltd.

Editor: Mark J. Sachner
Designer: Emma Randall
Production: John Lingham

Photo Credits:
Alamy: 11 (bottom), 12 (bottom), 29 (right), 31 (top); Cosmographics: 7, 9 (top); W. Disney/Everett/Rex: 11 (top); Istockphoto: 27; Moviestore Collection/Rex: 24–25; Public Domain: 9 (bottom), 10, 15 (top), 17 (bottom left), 22, 28, 29 (left); Shutterstock: Cover, 4–5, 6, 7 (bottom), 8, 12–13, 14–15, 16, 17 (bottom right), 18 (meunierd), 19, 20–21, 23, 24 (bottom), 25 (bottom), 26, 31 (bottom).

Library of Congress Control Number: 2014920328

ISBN 978-1-909673-92-2

Printed and published in the United States of America

For further information including rights and permissions requests, please contact our Customer Service Department at 877-337-8577.

Contents

The Black Flag

The year is 1700. It's a hot afternoon on a calm sea. A **merchant ship** loaded with treasure is heading for Spain from the Caribbean Sea.

Suddenly, the ship's lookout sees something in the distance. Is it another merchant ship? Or is it a ship carrying a crew of men who will fight, torture, and murder to get their hands on treasure?

That question is soon answered.
The distant ship raises a black flag.
Pirates!

The large, heavy merchant ship tries
to escape, but it is doomed. It will never
outrun the sleek, fast pirate ship....

Pirates have sailed the world's oceans for thousands of years.

For around 300 years, large numbers of pirates terrorized ships in the Caribbean. They also hunted for merchant ships around the coasts of North and South America.

Pirates became interested in the Americas in the early 1500s. At this time, explorers sailed from Europe to South America and the islands of the Caribbean. These explorers found vast quantities of gold and jewels in Peru. In Bolivia, they discovered a mountain that contained enormous amounts of silver. The explorers worked for the Spanish royal family, so they claimed the land and its treasures for Spain.

NORTH
AMERICA

Atlantic
Ocean

Caribbean Islands

Pacific Ocean

N

W   E

S

SOUTH
AMERICA

Peru

Bolivia

As more land was explored in the Americas, more people came from Spain. They set up **colonies** in North America, South America, and the Caribbean.

The Spanish settlers forced native people to work in mines gathering gold, silver, and jewels. Then these treasures were sent back to Spain on large ships.

People from other European nations, such as France and the Netherlands, also came to the Caribbean. They set up plantations to grow tobacco and sugar. These goods were then sent back to Europe. Soldiers and settlers from England also sailed to North America and the Caribbean to set up colonies.

Pirates didn't only attack a ship for its cargo. They also robbed passengers of their money and jewelry.

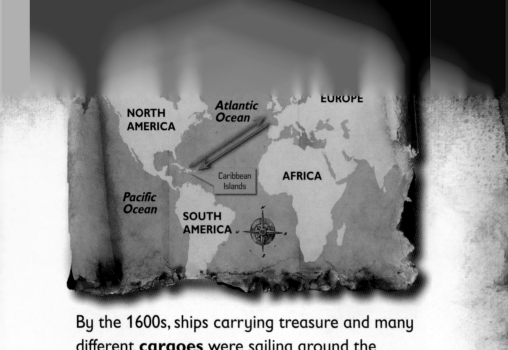

NORTH
AMERICA

*Atlantic
Ocean*

EUROPE

Caribbean
Islands

AFRICA

*Pacific
Ocean*

SOUTH
AMERICA

By the 1600s, ships carrying treasure and many different **cargoes** were sailing around the Caribbean. It was too much for pirates to resist!

Treasure was carried back to Spain in ships called galleons. Pirates sailed in galleons, too. This ship is a replica, or copy, of a galleon from the 1600s.

Choosing a Pirate's Life

Many Caribbean pirates were sailors who once sailed on merchant ships.

Even for experienced sailors, however, life at sea was hard work for little pay. A large merchant ship might have just 10 sailors aboard to run the ship. Captains often bullied and beat their men.

A pirate ship sometimes had a crew of 100 men to share the work. Pirates also had the chance to become rich. When a merchant ship was attacked by pirates, many sailors chose to join their attackers. The choice between death or a life of crime was an easy one!

Old records tell of just two female Caribbean pirates, named Anne Bonny and Mary Read. They sailed with a pirate captain named Calico Jack.

A Caribbean pirate crew might include men from many different countries. Some African pirates were runaway slaves. They had escaped from plantations on islands in the Caribbean.

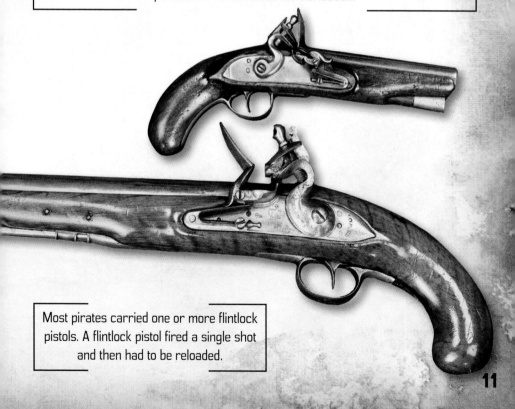

Most pirates carried one or more flintlock pistols. A flintlock pistol fired a single shot and then had to be reloaded.

Pirate Captains and Ships

The crew of a pirate ship was led by its captain.

A pirate crew often chose their captain by voting.
This was a gentlemanly way to decide who would lead
them. At other times, however, pirates were anything
but **civilized**!

Pirates could be lazy and **rebellious**. They were often
drunk, which led to arguments and fights. A pirate
captain had to be tough and **ruthless** to control the
men. He also had to find the crew lots of ships to attack.

Pirates in the Caribbean traveled in sailing ships
armed with 30 to 40 large guns that fired cannonballs.
A merchant ship, however, might have just 10 guns to
defend itself.

If a pirate captain did
a bad job, the crew
might rebel and vote
to replace him!

Sometimes a pirate captain attacked a ship that was faster or in better condition than his own. Then he stole the ship as well as its cargo!

A ship's gun

A cannonball

"No prey. No pay." This was a rule pirates lived by. It meant they only got paid if they captured treasure or other cargo. For a Caribbean pirate, a Spanish treasure ship was the ultimate prize!

Before being sent from South America to Spain, gold and silver were made into coins. Along with the valuable coins, treasure ships carried emeralds, pearls, and other precious gemstones. The cargo of a treasure ship would be worth millions of dollars in today's money.

Gold coins were called doubloons.

Because pirates were "wanted" men, they usually couldn't just stroll into harbor towns to get supplies. So when they attacked other ships, they also stole useful items. They took guns, barrels of gunpowder, pistols, ropes, sails, and carpentry tools.

were known as pieces of eight.

Pirates stole food, wine, brandy, and even barrels of fresh water from their victims.

The Pirate Code

Pirates lived by a code of equality and brotherhood.

Every pirate crew agreed on the rules for life aboard their ship. They also agreed on how any treasure would be divided. The rules were then written in an agreement called a set of articles.
Each crew member signed the agreement.

Any pirate who kept treasure just for himself was marooned, or left behind, on a deserted island.

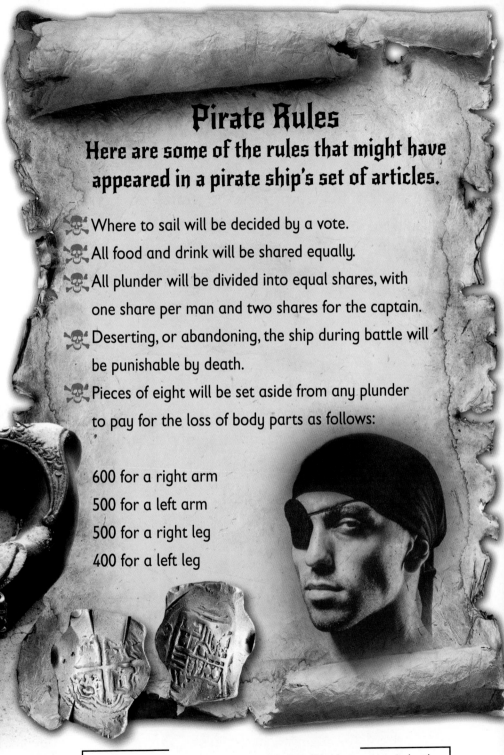

Pirate Rules

Here are some of the rules that might have appeared in a pirate ship's set of articles.

☠ Where to sail will be decided by a vote.

☠ All food and drink will be shared equally.

☠ All plunder will be divided into equal shares, with one share per man and two shares for the captain.

☠ Deserting, or abandoning, the ship during battle will be punishable by death.

☠ Pieces of eight will be set aside from any plunder to pay for the loss of body parts as follows:

600 for a right arm
500 for a left arm
500 for a right leg
400 for a left leg

A pirate might receive 100 pieces of eight if he lost an eye in battle.

Caribbean pirate ships cruised around the islands and coastlines of the Americas searching for ships to attack.

Most of the time, life for the pirates was pretty easy. They made repairs to the ship and mended sails. They played cards and games with dice. They also spent time eating and drinking large quantities of wine, brandy, and rum.

When supplies ran low, the ship dropped anchor close to a remote island. Then the pirates went ashore to collect fresh water and firewood for the **galley** stove. They also hunted for goats, wild pigs, birds, fish, and sea turtles. The fatty green flesh of a sea turtle was a favorite food.

Pirates didn't wash very often. Most of them had just one set of clothes that they wore day and night.

Pirates sometimes captured parrots as pets. The birds were easy and fun to care for and could be taught to speak. Parrots could also be sold for high prices in markets in London.

Scurvy, Boils, and Wooden Legs

A crowded ship filled with unwashed pirates smelled bad. Even worse, it was a very unhealthy place. The men often became sick with infections and diseases.

One of the most terrible diseases aboard ships was scurvy. A pirate with scurvy broke out in boils. His gums became jelly-like, and his teeth fell out. Before the victim died, his arms and legs swelled up and turned black.

Scurvy is caused by a lack of vitamin C. This vitamin is found in fruits and vegetables. Pirates and other sailors often ate no fresh produce.

Pirates were often badly injured during battles. If a man's leg or arm was torn apart by gunshot, it would usually have to be cut off. Many pirate ships had no doctor on board, though. So the ship's carpenter cut off the damaged limb with his woodworking tools! If a pirate survived having a leg cut off, he might replace his missing limb with a wooden leg.

Surrender or Fight?

Once pirates spotted a treasure or merchant ship, they raised their black or blood-red flag. The pirates' flag was designed to strike fear into the hearts of their victims.

Often the terrified crew of a merchant ship **surrendered** immediately. The men knew they might be outnumbered 10 to one. Sometimes, however, a merchant ship's crew fought back. Then the pirates showed no mercy.

Pirate flags used symbols such as the skull and crossbones, skeletons, swords, and bleeding hearts. The skull and crossbones was originally used in the log books, or records, of ships. The symbol showed there had been a death on board.

Pirates fired cannonballs, iron shot, and even old nails from their ship's many guns. They made hand grenades from hollow iron or wood balls filled with gunpowder. Once a grenade's fuse was lit, it was thrown onto a merchant ship's deck. Then it exploded among the sailors.

Under Attack!

Once pirates captured a merchant ship, they would invade and board it.

Sometimes they threw grappling hooks connected to ropes at the ship. Once the hooks dug into the merchant ship, the pirates used the ropes to climb aboard.

Old stories from sailors in the Caribbean tell of pirates cursing and swearing as they attacked like demons. The pirates fired their flintlock pistols and slashed at their victims with swords.

A rope and grappling hook

Pirates wanted the answer to just one question. Where was the treasure? Sometimes, they suspected that a ship's crew was hiding valuable goods. Then the pirates used torture to get the sailors to give up their treasure!

Pirates carried swords called cutlasses. A cutlass was about 2 feet (61 cm) long and had a curved blade.

Terrible Crimes

The methods of torture used by pirates to make their victims talk were horrific.

The pirates might begin by tying up a ship's captain or a sailor. Then they held lighted matches to the man's eyeballs. Or they might wind some rope around the victim's head. Then they pulled the ends of the rope tighter and tighter, until the man's eyes burst out of his skull. This ghastly form of torture was called "woolding."

Pirates wanted stories of their dreadful acts to spread among sailors. Then the crews of merchant ships were more likely to surrender without a fight.

Pirates might also whip a man, cut off his ears, or use him for target practice.

Some pirates carried
up to six pistols tied to
their belts. This allowed
a pirate to take more
shots. And it made
him look even more
threatening!

By the year 1720, there were about 2,000 pirates attacking ships in the Americas. Heavily armed warships sailed from Britain to hunt them down.

Once a pirate ship was captured, the men were put on trial. The sentence for piracy was death by hanging.

This painting shows the English pirate Blackbeard (Edward Teach) and his crew. They are fighting with men from the British navy during their capture in 1718.

This old illustration shows the body of the Scottish pirate Captain William Kidd hung in chains.

This model shows Blackbeard's head hung from the navy ship *HMS Pearl*.

After his execution, a pirate's body might be "hung in chains." This meant it was placed in a cage made of iron hoops and chains. Then the **corpse** was hung up in a harbor as a warning to others. Any man sailing in and out of the harbor would see the gruesome, rotting corpse. He would know that a pirate's life of crime doesn't pay!

Glossary

cargo (KAR-goh)
The goods carried on a ship, plane, or truck.

civilized (SIV-uh-lized)
Polite, courteous, or well-mannered.

colony (KAH-luh-nee)
An area that has been settled by people from another country and is ruled by that country.

corpse (KORPSS)
A dead human body.

galley (GAL-ee)
A kitchen on a boat or plane.

merchant ship (MUR-chint SHIP)
A ship that transports cargo or passengers. The ship is privately operated, and its owners are paid for the transportation services they provide.

rebellious (ri-BEL-yus)
Refusing to take orders from a person in charge, such as a ship's captain, and refusing to follow rules.

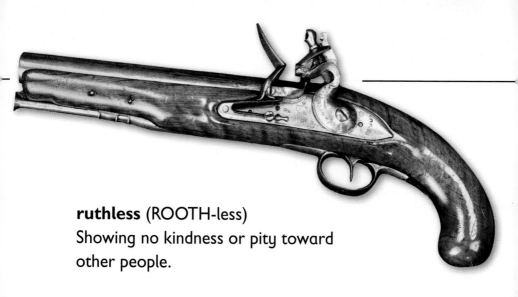

ruthless (ROOTH-less)
Showing no kindness or pity toward other people.

surrender (sur-EN-dur)
To give in or give up control to an opponent.

Index

Read More

Croce, Pat. *Blackbeard*.
Philadelphia: Running Press Kids
(2011).

Platt, Richard. *Pirate
(DK Eyewitness Books)*. New York:
DK Publishing (2007).

Learn More Online

To learn more about pirates, go to
www.rubytuesdaybooks.com/pirate